Shadow Shadow

Also by Roger Weingarten

POETRY

Tables of the Meridian (1982)
The Love & Death Boy (1981)
The Vermont Suicides (1978)
Ethan Benjamin Boldt (1975)
What are Birds Worth (1975)

ANTHOLOGIES

New American Poets of the '80s,
edited with Jack Myers (1984)
Love Stories, Love Poems,
edited with Joe David Bellamy (1982)

SHADOW
SHADOW

POEMS BY

Roger Weingarten

David R. Godine · Publisher
Boston

First published in 1986 by
David R. Godine, Publisher, Inc.
Horticultural Hall
300 Massachusetts Avenue
Boston, Massachusetts 02115

Copyright © 1986 by Roger Weingarten
Jacket illustration, "Le Gris et la Cote" by Paul Klee,
copyright © 1986 by Cosmopress, Geneva/A.D.A.G.P., Paris/Vaga, New York.

All rights reserved. No part of this book may be used
or reproduced in any manner whatsoever without written
permission, except in the case of brief quotations
embodied in critical articles and reviews.

Library of Congress Cataloging in Publication Data
Weingarten, Roger.
Shadow shadow.
I. Title.
PS3573.E3957S53 1986   811'.54   86-4691
ISBN 0-87923-634-5
ISBN 0-87923-635-3 (pbk.)

FIRST EDITION
Printed in the United States of America

For Ellen

Acknowledgment is gratefully made to the following periodicals:

The Antioch Review, Blue Buildings, Crazy Horse, The Missouri Review, New Letters, North American Review, Poetry Miscellany, Porch, Shenandoah, Southern Poetry Review, The Seneca Review, The Sewanee Review, and *Tendril.*

"Sometimes, at 36" originally appeared in *The New Yorker.*

"A Late Twentieth Century Afternoon with the Dead"; "Apples"; "Clay Tenements"; "It's Like That"; "Memoir"; "My Brain Tumor"; "New Year's, Montpelier, 1885"; "Not Quite a Love Poem"; "Premature Elegy by Firelight"; "Shadow Shadow"; "Tunnel Effect"; "Under the Wine Tree at the Edge of Desire"; and "Victorian Bacchanal" originally appeared in *Poetry.*

Ten poems appeared in a limited edition, *The Love & Death Boy,* published by W.D. Hoffstadt & Sons.

"Northern Lights" appeared in *Light Year '85.*

My thanks to Robert Long for his help in shaping the manuscript.

Heartfelt thanks to the Ingram Merrill Foundation for its support, and to Norwich University for a Dana Fellowship.

Contents

Under the Wine Tree at the Edge of Desire

- 3   *Apples*
- 5   *The Castrato of Moon Mash*
- 6   *Brass Rose Elegy*
- 8   *Not Quite a Love Poem*
- 9   *Memoir*
- 11 *Butchersgarden*
- 12 *Under the Wine Tree at the Edge of Desire*
- 14 *Victorian Bacchanal*
- 16 *Medium Walking the Sea of Serenity*

The Young: The Shadow: The Farewell

- 21 *Sometimes, at 36*
- 22 *Border Minstrel*
- 24 *Tunnel Effect*
- 26 *Spillway*
- 27 *Two Sons Drowning*
- 28 *Life Drawing in El Dorado*
- 30 *Nine Doors from the Kitchen*
- 32 *The Young: The Shadow: The Farewell*

Clay Tenements

- 39 *Quicksilver Shadow of a Dragonfly*
- 41 *Brown Velvet Coast*
- 42 *The Night-Blooming Cereus*
- 44 *Dear Roger*
- 46 *At the Grave of the 120-Year-Old Man*
- 47 *Epistolary*
- 49 *My Brain Tumor*
- 51 *Clay Tenements*

Welcome to the Encyclopedia of Thieves

- 55   Shadow Shadow
- 57   Gulf Stream
- 58   The Southern Nights
- 60   New Year's, Montpelier, 1885
- 62   Welcome to the Encyclopedia of Thieves
- 64   Eating the Angel of Death on Mt. Katahdin
- 66   My Uncle Brian's Concession
- 68   Northern Lights

Premature Elegy by Firelight

- 73   The Story of My Life
- 75   A Late Twentieth Century Afternoon with the Dead
- 77   Personal Holiday
- 81   Invisible Fire
- 83   Everytime You Say Yes It's an Indictment of the Last Six Months of My Life
- 84   Water Music
- 87   Premature Elegy by Firelight
- 88   It's Like That

*Under the Wine Tree
at the Edge of Desire*

Apples

I would forget to eat
regular meals or finish sentences
speaking to myself or a friend

over the business end of a two-man saw.
After a Mexican divorce, I built a house
in a small clearing, breaking ground

in mid-August, when a local orchard
kept me alive with Yellow Transparents
and Paula Reds. Out of a willow-strip

bushel basket, I'd clear the sawdust,
bring one to a polish on my canvas apron
and carry on until I couldn't see

the nail head or the stems
as I flipped them between vertical studs
into milkweed. The house burned

to nothing. The memory of a brass
plumb bob that caught the morning light
swaying from a rafter

little more this evening than a twinge
in the shinbone I tapped
with a hammer. But I can still taste

Seek No Further, Sheepsnose, Roxbury
Russet and that one reeling
monk of a Winesap crossing my eyes

into a poacher's ecstasy
passing a morning on a mattress
of dry leaves. If I were a worm

I'd tunnel into the core, curl up
and dream that I was the first
Red Delicious to cultivate the concupiscent

eye of the woman who wrote the first
independent clause in the history of love.
If I were the world, I'd metamorphose

into the mature ovary
of an apple tree, into the almond-sweet
cyanide of its seed, into its vermilion

red envelope, into the snowstorm
of its hard flesh, and rot
in the palm of God's hand

as He regards His handiwork
breaking up into continents, sinking
into oceans, with no little satisfaction,

awe and lust *si señor*.

The Castrato of Moon Mash

I pour my tea
over a slice of lime.

Blinded
by steam, I listen

to the hiss and crack
of ice cubes. And the pink

one-legged bird
preening itself

under cactus
painted on the frosted glass

shatters.
I'm on the wagon.

I'm in love
And I'll have another.

Brass Rose Elegy

I walk on my shadow and lean my elbows
into the hedge and stare obliquely,
like sorcery, up into the open
half-window, where, thin as oil

on water and olive-dark, he dresses
and squints at the hot morning
pressing, like pentimento,
through the dulse-colored leaves.

Barely a woman
Mother would tuck a sprig
of rosemary into her corset
and agree with the undefeated

standing armies of the ancient monarchs,
travelling the outskirts of our village,
that it would be slightly better
to open her legs for all concerned

on that green patch covered by tide
than to watch the little bones
of her feet scatter like deer hair
to the four winds. Turning around

I spread the pleated fan of my skirt
over the fold of my shadow—that lilac
son of a constant bicker and gaping
at my adolescence. I didn't butcher and slide

him under the bittersweet green revenge
of a berry bush, but almost. What kind
of a man isn't a father, but almost?
I listen to the flying

report of bees touching down
on goose flesh, almost lunar and pulling
against the grain of her arms, my veins,
where the starved sorcery of my blood

streaks to the blossom tinged with the quietly
lapping pulse of fratricide. Brother,
now that you're so inclined and dressed
to the throat like a loose-jointed

young man poling a barge, festooned
with bachelors, heroes, and youth, come sit
by this meadow beside water and a hedge
and put your hand to the flower.

Not Quite a Love Poem

There was that early evening
scene in the street: a bearded man

in a windbreaker leaning into the blue
car window, a black-haired woman

crying at the wheel and the soft
ripple of a boy's mouth

quietly orbiting. While the court
janitor watched from the steps

he turned up the volume on his earphones
and puckered his lips

at the bystanders gathering under streetlight
that flickers into night. In the naugahyde

red booth of a coffee shop, over butter
wrappers and sweet rolls, she tore into the white

underbelly of his forearm, then he
squeezed her fists into bruises

when she went for his face, stretching
over the table, the black pepper

of her hair spilling. Then again,
after threats, witnesses, and a lawyer's blue

tattooed earlobe shuffle off to xerox
the signed agreement, they held

each other in bronze between diplomas
on the wall and potted ferns, not knowing

what was over or what had just begun.

Memoir

You again. The ecstatic posture. The victory symbol
around a cigarette, leaning
primeval into the carved
hotel headboard, your wrists without bracelets
enthroned on your knees, while twenty-one stories
above New York, you say I

don't like sex. The cab
pulls away from the pier. Because the driver
asks how I could leave such a woman, I turn
around again to your wine-
red blouse, and the curve of your chin
shadowed in the sunlit-yellow

sky of your hair. I had just come down
with mononucleosis and a new car: In the black
and chrome interior we were delivering
ourselves under the rounded niche of a maple
in the corner lot
of your parents' church when the connection
between the flying buttresses and our encroachment
on the marginal regions—walking toward us,
taking us in, as if we
were even younger and stabbing a puppy—drops
a pencil-written parking ticket
through the slit in the mist.
An elegant old man
in a squash hat and the top half

of a child's head are staring at you
through the plate glass of Budin's
Delicatessen: Kaplansky, daydreamer,
minus a forefinger, steps
from the meat counter pinching
plates of corned beef steaming on the heel. He deals them
across the chrome-rimmed

formica table, wipes his hands,
looking at me deadpan, on that bedsheet
of an apron, backtracks

through sawdust
for our side order of canoe-shaped
dills floating in brine. The wind,
coming down from Canada, hard
off the green ice of Lake Erie,
and swirling in snow,
whips the hat into the cobalt dark,
the door open, and the tracks
into the oblivion we've both been waiting for.

Butchersgarden

I track the belly down
spread the twisting
coarse hairs into the black
wings of a butterfly
put my lips to the butter
and spread lord our pleasure
across the diminutive blue
ravines of her thighs up
into the roiling
thumb and forefinger the son
and daughter of my right hand
as
for the world momentarily
concealed under the lush oriental
weave of little deaths and ecstasy dear
jesus when will your kneeling swaying
and ever humble servant ever care
to tuck his left hand under
the braided fringe and pull the latch
and tumble into the daylit mica-thin
hunter's butcher's solipsist's
cocoon where I eat myself
alive waiting.

Under the Wine Tree at the Edge of Desire

> *Perhaps the essence of being a Jew meant to live forever in a state of expectation for that which would not come.*—Irving Howe

The two of them whispering in a hot breath
about themselves—bibbed
in nasturtium red

and blue scarves and wearing the overall sunburn
of middle age in the provinces—scrape,
with their fingernails, an impasto

of olive oil, salt, and shattered garlic
across the torn, bone-white loaves, as large
as the thigh being scrubbed

raw by a woman bending with the alders
over the river framed
in the half-shaded glass. Hands that

have forged iron shoes and railings, forged themselves
out of white scars and rust, like a ball of roots, dig
for the cold snack, reappear, break its back, and paint

the quiet areas. *El revisor*—his neck
cross-hatched with the fine canals of age, the surging
force choking vermilion under all

that uniform, and the sagging
pepper and salt picket fence of mustache
smashed against his cheek—slides

the compartment door. Anxiety
and memory: those little valves
open like the red skirts of wine, thick and sharp

as an aged cheddar, we hoisted into the half-dark
outline of the gabled roof, leaning back
into the headboard, and wearing a quilt for a quickly

dissolving six years. Brush and twigs
sweep along the water, predictable as the cigarette
ash, absent-mindedly long and falling

off my knee to the carpeting
of wine and chicken bones. I seize
el revisor by the wrist: *Donde esta una ventanilla*

abierta? Plunging
up to my neck into the hard air that sweeps
the tears and my last ballpoint from behind my ear

leaving the red cactus flower
hedges of Almeria and a railroad worker
holding up the sun with an upside-down, dark-green

glass jug of desire to his lips, another
pissing like an archangel over the edge
of a ravine, while the third, clean-

shaven and pointing, screams, *la barba, la barba*
at the sight of my scarlet and brown
high relief, cold and sucking air

toward Alicante.

Victorian Bacchanal

A red granite flame
burst
from the leaf-shaped
malachite urn
that embellishes a balustrade
above the facade of black and white
marble triangles and open space
held up
by a leaded window
sash through which, in wet shoes,
I look out over the irregular, cracked
slate tiles balanced in the invisible
open palms of a dozen stoop-shouldered
half-nude, dark
yellow giants that form
a colonnade, under which
a man's disposition—
that fell to your lot—
and the memory of its cruelty,
that never forgave itself,
ricochet
off the stone bellies
that I will to tense
and crumble against the reservoir
of marrow in his knuckles, retired
in the belief that if they
even graze your cheek, you will
speak with your heels: standing
here in this
mahogany palace, wanting you to leave
his pleasure in the military,
on duty outside the topiary
labyrinth of formal gardens, their blue
steel barrels
up their sleeves, overhead

and rising toward my desire
to have you—radiant
gentle friend and poet—
join what remains
unfinished: our journey toward
the uncomplicated
grateful polygamy of old age.

Medium Walking the Sea of Serenity

I let go of my eyes and remembered
the windowshade you pulled so far
beneath the sill, I had to twist it, like paper

and tobacco, before it would rise above your hair
curled into pine shavings
under the sudden light.

Three months
after slipping with sunglasses through the backyard
shadow, so you, the neighbor

and her nose for musk and separation
couldn't see the double
eclipse of fear looking down

at my ankles, like distant cousins stepping
out of moccasins and not ready yet
to support the children, dodge through the trees

around a reservoir, or speak to a lawyer.
But I pushed words, gently, some said beautifully,
through the belly folding hazel

and sepia into itself for a life
my dearest friend pressed, for me,
into a lithograph. Letting go

of my feet, I said, if you ever hurt
me again—and then promotion, after twenty years,
slipped through your hand. You said, why poetry;

why school? You accused
me of being a mother. You snowed
my parents and swiveled the analyst

around in her chair; waxed the floor until my friends
could see themselves buried upside-down and staring
at the corridors of Christmas and the lights

over the sunken bath. To steel myself
against the pressure of your vigilance
over what kept me

after a party, the library, or lunch with a friend,
I secreted a shot glass, etc., into the excelsior
under the driver's seat. I let go of my hands.

A few friends, feverish with language, helped me
hypnotize myself into poetry. I gave them
what any woman pulling away from the tar

of one life with a stiff back and only
their vision of the next
could give; I sat there like a medium

waiting to speak. Listen. I put my ear
like a needle into the groove of your revolving,
matter-of-fact, detailed predictions

of my death, if I
should have nerve enough
and hear the bell and margin release

sliding into place for some
one or two imagined
in a coincidence of poems, who should,

with your permission, have lifted the safety
catch into a light
drizzle of bullets to play upon

the reason—At least
they would have seen me
letting go of that glass

cobweb of a body, your threat
against the children, and a future
serene with any man I didn't need

The Young:
The Shadow:
The Farewell

Sometimes, at Thirty-Six

I'm walking a side street
looking down at the pattern
of tiny deaths on the orange-and-mica
granite slabs that slope

into the river or nodding the bearded
geography of my head at the light gray
figures of the evening becoming paper
cut-outs pushing carts. Leaf season

overwhelms the sharp cheese, the year
of the near suicide and the amber
jewel bobbing in the applejack
and sometimes, approaching the half-

submerged railroad ties
rotting in the path to the quarry,
suffocated with leaves everywhere
gone yellow, I look up at the stained

fingers of my old friend yellow birch,
who had a fatal yen for gossip, heights,
and exported blends, and imagine
the two of us pacing that nun's cap

of a hill looking east at the soft-bellied
mountains, or heaving the bone-weary
branches high over the dark
brown water, and sharing smoke, an apple

gone soft in my pocket,
and quiet praise for the spirit
of poetry climbing on hands
and knees into middle age.

Border Minstrel

I enter the town disguised
as a stoop-shouldered friar

staring at his toes and passing
through fairground stalls and the hour

of the butcher bringing night.
I scale walls, free prisoners, down

the sheriff's beer and bind
his upside-down pig's bladder

of a figure to the tiniest
branch in the square of beggars

and pigeon feathers. I take
my leave and my time. Skip

rocks soft as the open
palm of a wife on the river

by light of fireflies and applause
of crickets who pause while my stone,

like a priest thrown
out of a tavern, reels and disappears.

I kneel to this wet mirage
slapping the bank, my lips dry and just

scratching the surface. And sense
a presence at the hairs

of my neck about to lunge, heave
to the side as sword followed by man

are swallowed by river. I remove disguise
and chain mail and dive

like a nightmare over the nearly
drowned ex-official of the crown.

I love to run surprise
like a razor across my face and climb

the high turrets of a cathedral
like a whisper. It's daybreak. I'll mend

the torn strap of my sandal with a thorn
and the green vine of the wild grape, sleep

like a prince in a meadow of mustard flowers
and least-weasels catching mice.

Who knows if anyone ever dies.
I'll be back.

Tunnel Effect

I wave to an old woman scooping water
from a cistern, and turn the corner
into a confusion of raw umber, sap-

green horseweed, and burrs that I push
from a sign, with a portable easel
and my usual excess of brushes, that reads

all vehicles at their own risk: Abandoned Road.
I look through two
rusty bullet holes at the secondhand

artery of another century—that might
well have been driven underground
or dredged out of the murk of the Mediterranean—

and the low, studded waves of clover
on either side. Two fencerows of osage orange,
with their green, brain-carved fruit,

and swamp-hickory stand at odd,
interlocking angles, like the groined
vaults of Norman architecture, over black

Iowa clay, gashed and rising
into moss-covered shoulders. Months later,
when I return with my winter easel

after freezing rain, it will become a crystal
highway of sienna twigs, emeralds,
and foliated serpentine. This time

I walk in and wait for my eyes to adjust
and follow the handle
of a frying pan off the road into an open grave

of farm machinery and bog willow
pushing through bedsprings. I chew
to the center of a berry concealing weevils

that bite my tongue as I begin
to climb out of sunlight and back
through the branches that hold the breeze

of Abandoned Road. When I see the outline
of a bird thrashing in leaves, I set
easel and paper down, and fold a wedge

of cardboard around a thick
cadmium orange and a blue
and squeeze them into the crowded shapes

of a love affair, dragging the wash to the mixed
gray rendering of my husband
and his wife. Out of the branches

that he parts to give me light, a one-eyed boy
with several muskrats over his back
looks over mine. While I, believing

this triangle of eyes was something more
down-to-earth than metaphor for the survival
techniques of imagination, put

finishing touches to the foliage, and the powder-
blue concentration of his iris
into the base color of a wet sky.

Spillway

Sliding the leaf-slippery bank to the twigs and rust
passing shallow under the overhanging
sheets of sycamore
bark, light, and thorny plumes
of blackberries, I nearly
collide with the stooped figure
of another boy poking around
after snails and rocks that fall
from the clay pipe of Shaker Lakes after a rain

into this ravine, deckle-edged with the cold
afternoon shadow cut into the exposed
half-alive mob of roots jutting out
like arms petrified in a lava flow. Thick lenses
magnify his irises into Jupiter rings. His lips purse
into the taut dignity of a line above green
and black plaid buttoned to the throat. He steps out
on a moss-polished rock, bends to the mystery,

slips, refuses my hand, and leaves
me to my
usual arrangement with the clay pipes: the play of water
trickling between the shoulder blades
of a daydream, hunkered
by the side of a creek until my legs
go stiff, drawing
nothing
with a green stick in the mud.

Two Sons Drowning

The bottom clawed out of a canvas boat,
a wave and a reef. I take the towheaded

struggling thief of my heart into the slippery
crook of my arm and the blue-faced

medicine man of my moods, his collar
between my teeth. And with a free hand

reach for the Adam's apple
laughing from a cloud that breathed

this scene into the unwilling
lungs of my dream, and try to crush

the larynx flailing until I wake in nightsweat,
that hand around my throat, teeth and arm

holding on to the legacy
of my father's love, looking

at the pregnant falling and rising
of my wife's belly under the sheet. I want

to wake her now, shake her arms, and say
what a thick-skinned, elusive stranger

I am to myself and the selves I meet
in the early light, as if I

were older, my own father, and sleeping next
to the son in me, and have her touch

the pulse climbing my neck, and say
forgive yourself, go back to sleep.

Life Drawing in El Dorado

Let's start in the barn with an old man's back
hunched against a bale of mixed grass. His sunlit

double chin appraises the silk-skinned long fingers
braiding corn and a scattering of cats, blood-red

onions and a basket of hollyhock tumbling
over each other in dust rising from the history

of iron wheels engraved like an accordion
across the floor. A young woman

scrubs beets in a wet sink between a press
of trees and a garden, her willow-

brown hair wound around the curve
of her ears. Her mother,

in the dooryard, mumbles the future
of grandchildren over a quick stream

of spinning wool. And they both see
in the pale moon of morning

husband or son-in-law stripped to the waist
and scraping down his trawler in the sweet

stink of the harbor, the tidal mud
curing in the cool late summer, and he

looks up at me, an itinerant painter
setting up easel and sable

paraphernalia of my trade, smiles
and calls to the shadow on its side

sleeping it off under a dinghy, then leans
a shoulder into his work like a child

milking a cow for warmth and privacy, his face
turned, scolding the lazy

sunfish-and-scrod-filled ocean, its floating islands
of dulse and rockweed.

Nine Doors from the Kitchen

It's true that I said, hello Grandpa
you son of a bitch, and he said
hold on a minute, here's Grandma, and I

pushed myself over the edge
of the pleasure of showing off, then she said,
where's Mother, who told her

I learned it from the gardener
turning the phrase with a scroll
of turf unraveling as I followed the green-

stained kneecaps of his overalls
across the magic. Even
if it's not absolutely

certain that I—unaccompanied
toilet-trained at an early age,
wishing everyone goodnight, goodnight—

closed the door, turning The Moondog
Hour on the radio, stood on the bed
and raised my colors into a sling

half-filled with meteorites that fell
overhead and around the wallpaper
constellations—it is

documented that, stealing away from a nursery
school feast of peanut butter
with a diaper of a different color, I leaped

up scaffolding and nearly airborne
finished my abstract impression
before I was collared. If Mother

was no longer amused, and if
she slid a plate into the gold-
speckled black linoleum, where I

was forever to stick my nose in it, I lose
in the confusion of a dream of kneeling
face-forward and surrounded

by great-aunts rising to argue
over which apple would yield the longest peel, until
encased in the shavings of pippins and McIntosh I woke

at twelve with a wooden match and the formula
for launching a rocket through the chimney. Nearly falling
out of a passenger seat, I reached for the curb

with the back of my fist, half-open and arcing
an orange over the Buick at a plaid
prep-school uniform, her ankles in white socks

back-pedaling down the boulevard against the slow-
motion, mesmerizing, counterclockwise, harvest
moon revolving in the spokes hallelujah

and she never stopped.

The Young: The Shadow: The Farewell

Father pushed the double edge
through the mirror in the medicine cabinet.

The boy in the attic under the steep roof
picked it up like a mousetail

and imagined Father, opening the door,
would laugh in his belly: What

have you got; what are you doing? Toy drums
up in flames, the fire chief pointed through the bars

with his fat thumb and said, if you do that
once more, I'll turn the lock

and eat the key. He beat the morning
to the front lawn, where his somnambulist

brother straddled a tricycle. The neighbor
called Mother to the window just

as they were coming down the hill, blue pastel
striped pajama bottoms tied

to the handlebars like kitetails and waving on
the sunrise. Out of the haze, a first poem—

Still as a pill/I give you a thrill—a greeting card
to Mother in his fifth year. Lit a match

to the dry weeds of a vacant lot, and dreamt
a great-bearded someone held him by his hair

over a sink, and cut his throat in the men's room
of a football stadium, wiped it clean

with St. Veronica's veil that
he had seen the old woman

unfold on a Sunday-morning
religious hour. Skipped fourth grade. Lost a friend

to an operation not quite perfected, whose sister,
walking to school, said that Steve's

up there. Squinting hard, he locked himself
in a stall, wouldn't go to class, and when he did

he cackled like an exotic bird or the tide
slapping rocks. He kicked around

with powdered charcoal,
sulfur,

and saltpeter. Chased butterflies
into the marsh. Wiped himself

with poison ivy after a sudden
shift in the wind. Read books. Wrote poems. Coiled

resentment like a slow worm around
what the tailor's lips, fanning out with pins, called

his snake hips, remembering
the white fossil and one whisker

stuck on the black and blue Gillette. Grandmother
buttered warm bagels and drove the children, falling

over the seat of her Pontiac, around the lake
to the amusement park. Aunt boiled a potato

salad that glowed
like an orange moon on the picnic table, yards

from where he waded in the creek
with cousins, their pants rolled

turban-fashion above their white knees under the drift
of a charcoal fire. His parents moved

three times in two years in the same town.
He took Hebrew from the mouth of a young owl

who slapped memory into knuckles with a high-polished
Star of David. An emergency operation, a bar mitzvah;

a girlfriend, painting a tree, walked backwards
off a cliff; his parents divorced; the lawyers

in their pelican jowls
surrounded him. Paddled for discipline, like Caesar's

children, he spent a weekend with his Latin teacher
and two other sets of eyes adjusting to the moonlit

dark path curving away from the cabin. He stole a car
and got caught. Moving like an argument

between apartments, he made
two friends, love, and the respect

of one teacher; envy, in a thin white belt,
wanted to grind him under a tap

screwed into a heel, who saw him talking
to himself and snapping his fingers. He tripped

over nothing in a parking lot, the groceries
cradled in either arm becoming

black holes, and woke up
steering a forklift through a summer job. Father

socked him in the chest
in the lightshadowed, warehouse air,

hardly there and stinking from the dead river.
He grabbed the fists, and squeezed them

until they both broke down, and he drove off
into a freshman year.

Clay Tenements

Quicksilver Shadow of a Dragonfly

She scrubbed her eyes with the heel of her palm.
Her knuckles stared down a corridor of draftees,
laughing at their thumbs or over their shoulders,
that began at the nape of the driver's neck
and ended under a luggage rack in saliva
burning her pariah's belly. And if she hadn't bathed

for awhile. If her hair knotted
like the argument of a desperate prayer
that described her reaching
for the foothills of middle age at twenty-three,
not even one violent band of muscle
trying to rebel against the maternal, small ark

of her rib cage, breathing deeply and traveling
to a draft physical. And then the rumored
anti-Semitism of boot camp instead of crossing,
with Quakers, the easier answer of the border
or the hall to the enlistment center. And if you,
a reader of poems, don't forgive

the ambiguity of her position—please,
don't worry about it: The yellow
corridor shot the bowstring
girder bridge and somersaulted once
into the beautifully random collection

of stones and river birds. Her parents, embarrassed
to the quick that their firstborn refused
to write popular novels or legal briefs,
issued her poems, posthumously, under my name.
A reviewer claimed they were intoxicated,
complicated, narrative as hell,

but the psychiatrist, nearly whispering
over a cast-iron skull with mice running in
and out of eye sockets, confided
that her second cousin had once
scribbled verse for a magazine. That I needn't
fret about a ghost walking forever

up a riverbed, what drugs I'd taken, or the foreign wars.
She asked if I knew my name, and passed
Valium and a bus coupon across the mahogany
under glass that compressed an iridescent
blue insect.

Brown Velvet Coast

An amphibious arcobat skips a shell
into the tide, launching a towel,

like a harlequin somersaulting
for royalty, over the prostrate

sandberries and their gradual drift
out of cattails, back

into the scattered lights of pleasure:
the dabs, the dots, the flickering

breakwall, where his eye
sails, a little drunk and agonized,

away from the wedding
at the whitewashed resort hotel.

A lighthouse, like quicksilver
on the promontory, pirouettes

with jealous eyes above the dark, luminous
unravelling over the endless suspirations

of imagination, desperate and cut
from its moorings, scudding along until

colliding with a horse's blue phosphorescence
breaking from the undertow, over

each other suddenly, as logs in fire,
or the husband

and wife that sweep each other
under the sycamore to music.

The Night-Blooming Cereus

When you spoke to me—wrapped in your faded, perennial,
black raincoat that embraced
the connective tissue to those shadowed,
meditative, mossy paths that laced the interior
of the Vermont woods, where we found each other leaning

over the railing of a rickety bridge, an amber
bottle tipped in the air, the neck
pressed and forming a vacuum around your tongue
in the stern of this: austere, beam-and-stucco
vaulting past the blue, all-

too-familiar stained-glass
figures of your youth, watching your father
gesture to his parishioners—you said that I, as unlikely
a friend and vice versa, am the only
one of them (You illustrate, tossing a prayer,

bound in black, the gold-rimmed pages
ruffling into swan-feathers) in twenty-odd years that you didn't
push away: if I arrived at a bus terminal, the dry
taste of sleep on my tongue, took a room
with a skylight and no windows, furnished

in the middle-class fashion, a corridor
and a kitchen that I could share with a semi-bald
Jehovah's Witness, my landlord, his atheist daughter
for a neighbor, and never left, I'd remember:
first, the cold maple pressing my heel into ice
uncrossing my feet over the back of that pew, then
the adolescent portrait
you drew of yourself: "In the high
polish of my Sunday shoes and a cranberry jacket, I could touch
the reflection of a man who could see all the way through

the architecture of his faith
to his son, the son of a nurse, who pursued me
through the rock-swollen catacombs of childhood, which I fled,
barefoot and half-asleep with poetry, up the wild
strawberry and dew-slick

hill of night, her arms shaking
like a corncrib being devoured by raccoons,
like brooms holding
up the moon, relentless and high into the New England
claustrophobia." In this weather

we left the six-pack, almost empty
and floating pre-natal
in its own liquid, inside
the baptismal font, one for the pastor. Years later,
in a town without weather, we were living

in cave-dark Siamese apartments, the wall we shared
white and thin as a moth wing, me
sleeping by night, and you by day; we kept a vigil,
someone always clearing their throat or tapping the keys
of a typewriter. Once you woke me
with a chocolate bar glowing in the vehement

yellow of a birthday candle; another time
to warn of a neighbor twisting
his wife's hair around his fist through the broken
window, and again to insist
that I stereotype you in my poems, proving
that I didn't love you.

Dear Roger

Write me a letter of recommendation. A concise
page about the years we were familiar
only academically. You needn't be concerned

with the nights I've disemboweled working the try-
your-strength machine, the cash desk at the junk stalls,
and the chair o' plane. If you need more

inside information, I've attached my resume: two
months there, two here—giving breath
to paper serpents, putting heads on beers—with all

I could carry on my lap, as itinerant, inward
and cynical as Cheap John's wardrobe of ageless
pickpockets and freaks. Love, by the sweet wine

of the Crucifixion, is as dead for me as the ragged
edge of the straight razor climbing your throat.
I must develop additional competencies

in chemistry and soil science. I want to brush
my canines in anhydrous ammonia, to hire myself
out as a farmhand with a Ph.D., pivoting

out of a midway pleasance snapshot of me in straw
and a bow tie, lifting Old Reb by nicotine-stained
fingers growing out of his shoulders, like the epaulets

of a good soldier. If this letter, high-stepping
a water balloon out of the free-
throw area up to the basket, doesn't wash

all the distortions of guilt and memory out of a past
that needn't concern you; if it doesn't typecast
you-as-anything more than a blindfolded

automatic fortuneteller under glass, and singe
the very hairs off the tunic of your imagination, or inquire
beyond the state of your health—ready to secede

or surrendering—or recollect the manuscript you suffocated
accidentally, I don't apologize; I don't care
if all the oily sonnets in Rumania shred in the windmills,

if our shitkicking old cronies never break
another line or treaty with the tribes of Margarita
and Muscatel . . . I'm sure

you get my drift and that your second nature
knows the ins and outs of an invincible light
cavalry charge of words recommending me

to the acting chair of agricultural
engineering. Send it, and this self-addressed
stamped postcard to reassure me—suspended here

like a Zionist in a pyramid—of your quick dispatch.
Again, I hope this letter finds you in good repair.
Take care. As ever. Sincerely yours.

At the Grave of the 120-Year-Old Man

I touch the high white forehead of your headstone
with disbelief: How could anyone survive
that many sermons, blackfly seasons, or the double
row of wives and children impaled on either side
of your will to look up and around the table
after another "our Father" at another
family gathering raising
their eyes under the silver maple
shading other tablets that command
more respect for the longevity
of what makes them stone, slate-black
and gray, than for a nearly
nameless citizen of the northeast kingdom
who outlives one century and a good piece
of another. The Onion River running
between your grave and the overarching
willow and river birch
understands why someone leans over me like a bursting
patriarchal light, much better than I
why the cold remains of your need
to hang on held until the pall of unresolved
misery radiated over the fallen and crumbling markers
of others who knew better. Neighbor,
I'm going home for a sledgehammer and a flask
of salt water to break your stone into eternity
after I wet it down proper, spit
in the river to get the taste of unworthiness out of my mouth,
   then
I'm walking backwards to feed one I love
a lifetime of this mortal flesh today
until all that remains is salt
in her mouth.

Epistolary

The steam from their nostrils climbed
out of the valley of fireflies. There were no curves.

The conifers guarded the night like an infantry
of jealous husbands. At mountaintop, the coachman

tossed the mail with a curse, lashed the air
without giving his team a catch of breath,

white-lathered, and their eyes
reflecting the water-swollen, orange

midsummer moon that passed through a window
and illuminated the sole-passengers: A stoop-shouldered,

bearded serial-novelist, outfitted
in the three-piece, dark haberdashery

of his era, watch and fob, tumbling
with apologies into the lap of an impressionable

woman in a cape, a mother of three,
she said, whose silent

displeasure with her domestic state of affairs
made her sad, desirable, and agree

to correspond through a trusted half sister
in Randolph, but she went for his wrist

before he pulled the shade, sat back
and recollected himself as a boy, lazy

and nested in a crater of gnarled roots
poking the tip of a bamboo

at the floating antennae of the yellow mudwasp
floating in the pond. A woman as fragile

and transparent as honey emerged
out of the brush and milkweed, so close he ran

his adolescent fingers down her calf. Her face,
without expression, broke the surface

into an evolution of ripples, which a man,
like a star, reckless

and falling through the atmosphere, found
inevitable, and blue, and disappeared.

My Brain Tumor

I stepped into his cranium like a rumor
of things vaguely desired, not quite
understood or anticipated. I fit right in
and made the kind of hardworking
impression the big toe of a ballerina
makes on a shoe, beginning to see that I
was really wanted in ways I hadn't been
before. We got engaged,
blood tests and a quick ceremony in the reform
rabbi's study of spiked punch, party lights,
and psychedelics. We had kids
that look like my maternal grandparents
and grew into the family business or left
for parts not completely unknown. Then one
blue cerebral night we fought like praying
mantises: He brought strangers
into the argument but I
remained aloof, writing only
to the morning paper's religious column
under a nom de plume: Dear Mary
Magdalene: He is more to me
than life, but I could kill him for poking
into my diary—what do a few premarital
quickies matter to a love like ours. Please
for the love of Jesus help us. Desperately yours,
Marge Tolstoy. But,
before she could answer, he had me
removed and immortalized in a large jar
of formaldehyde he keeps by his side, even
when he curls under blankets pretending to sleep.
Like the Strategic Air Command
patrolling the Dew Line, I keep a vigil
over time itself, you might say if you
were waxing philosophical about my little
Eichmann ship in a bottle glass

paperweight without snow. O
God isn't dead enough for my money. The hell
with intellectual men and the milky way
over Nevada. I'm going to climb to the very
top of the world's tallest water-towers
and spray-paint our love in tongues
of flame from Needles, California,
to Pittsburgh, so he
can see it in his sleep, driving hard
across America, splitting gears
and hairs in his worst dreams, and whispering
into his pillow how he misses me.

Clay Tenements

Under the date palms, the red mission
tile roofs, and the bamboo
lean-to shading the carports
he works the neighborhood. Rifling the purse
between the pink and easy
arms of a chair, his eyes, inlaid
above gaunt, jutting bones

sweep the meaningless
bric-a-brac across the mantle. And small change
on the vanity in the house next door—except
a buffalo-head nickel
that vanishes under a bed—slides
like the cellophane
skeletons of June bugs
sucked dry by a spider feeding at night
into the undercurrent of his silk maroon
shirt pocket. Miles across the endless
southwestern sprawl, behind bars,
and not pressing his elbows into his thighs, there sits
an officer of the Department of Defense, who sees,
I hope forever, himself emptying a revolver
he claimed was there for his own
wish for self-destruction
into his wife, who believed in a gentle word,
a little privacy to dream and write, *please
don't*, who looked up
through the gray shallows
of uniformed life and beyond
the first words of a poem that embraced
the domestic silences of neighbors,
wives themselves, craning their necks
at the collision of a jet stream and a dust devil
over a military base, breaking up
into the debris-speckled

detail of the future. Having
threatened his children, having confessed, he revealed
no remorse at resolving the sudden
marital and occupational hazards
of middle age, an air force
gunner turning
inward, swarming outward, and strafing
the potted cactus and oak parquet. On grass-
stained knees, in the neighborhood of the rifler
    of purses, another
whose home is being relieved
of its material burden, presses the Dutch
bulbs into the soil, and weeps
in her belly for the loss of her friend, and her own
long-remembered close call after a black-and-blue
sunrise.

*Welcome to the
Encylopedia of Thieves*

Shadow Shadow

I, too, once spouted yards of poetry, and rushed
the sunrise into my sister's giggle, slamming the door
of one chamber into another until my father, rabbi
of the only synagogue in the Berkshires, collared us
by the scruff and swore
there would be no honey cake if we
woke Mother (two of her could have sailed
to America in Emily's housedress) the smell of schnapps
hovering in his beard's underbrush. I
never hung back at the top of the stairwell, drawing
pictures in my head of anyone's
parlor shenanigans, *especially*

my father's, who firmly said never to pisch
pardon his Yiddish, in the pot you eat from, but like her
my intensity gathered in my belly,
the hearth, the staircase
spiraling to cupola, where I cried and choked
on father's refusal to bless
my first marriage: You remember that northwest
window in our room? Where Emily
lowered ginger
and almond cookies to the little ones squinting
up at the sun and reaching for the shadow
that became a bride lowering herself on old shoestrings
braided for strength and magic

out of that white whale of a house, no velvet
neckpiece to set off the mixture of fear
and desire glazing my wide, brown irises—not yet
puffed and diminished into wrinkles, or mocked
by rouged dark bags of tears I've held in check
in case you, or any young man with a pen
or tape recorder would break the dry
monotony of this retirement

city named for the sun, without an oak or little ones
to carve the acorns for Halloween; the sun
my second husband willed to me
after scattering ashes into wind
that slapped a few white fragments back in my face. Emily
and I share a secret. We knew the same loose board, nearly
equidistant from the stove and closet
where the curators display her dress. There was a poem
folded twice; so bitter; so simple.
I put it to memory. It became—like a lapis lazuli

scarab carved by some ancient Hebrew craftsman
and welded by time to the breastbone
of a pharoah—our poem. Breaking faith, if I let it go.
However, I'll tell you this: You are young; you have
my father's mouth; his high forehead, wrinkled and glowing
stain in the night, and absolutely
no one gradually withdraws from life. Someone inside,
like a seed breaking free of the groundfallen fruit,
puts out her own
taproot like a wing, and either flies or doesn't.
We didn't. It was all a dream. Linen or gabardine.

Gulf Stream

Coming across the bottomland of Washington County
under the canopy of a Blue Seal Feeds

sun visor, his one good ear
plugged above the death

rattle of a John Deere tractor
trailing a spray of well water and a defoliant

dropped out of the cumulus
sky of another land, he hears tunes

and Paul Harvey over the radio. Beneath the topsoil
and a plug of chewing tobacco, a bridge of tiles

guides the runoff into Old Man's Creek, over which,
on New Year's Eve, he and I will climb—

out of breath and ice—after his brown
and white heifers heading for the cemetery

his youngest boy clears of poison ivy
and witchgrass with a scythe. Afterwards, his wife

will come into the barn with a pail
of steamed corn and sandwiches. Mud season's

Old Man's Creek is a dairy farmer
unable to stand the sight of another

summer horizon becoming the chill
factor of January, who rushes for the gray dancing

foam of the river that headlong feeds
the Mississippi just north and to the east

of nowhere and Hart Crane.

The Southern Nights

Not easily lured by the flickering
elm's burning torso illuminating
the masked bandits of Louisa County
coming en masse down the lane to climb

the red slats of a corncrib
toward a gibbous moon turning a cloud
behind the windmill into a brown
recluse spider, I believe

the secret of my husband's ambition
is locked in a copper-lined
tobacco cabinet having a cigarette
in the easy chair, Tolstoy's

dog-eared *Kreutzer Sonata* open
across his thigh: Like interwoven
twin cocoons, a man on a train
must tell his story to a stranger. He

brings down the shade on the profile of my Missouri
meerschaum smouldering
sinsemilla on the porch, pulls the chain
on the reading lamp, and contemplates divorce. I

am not put out that the newspaper mulch
weighted down with clods between cornflowers
and red-leafed spinach has been pushed aside
by volunteers; not panicked
that our landlord, oil-stained and quick to laugh

at old jokes, is here
to ignite a pyramid of tractor tires, upwind
of our bedroom window, where the peafowl,
settled for the night, come screaming

above the immensity of linden branches
brimming over these peeled, rickety boards
I can see in the dark
glow of what will soon be

the special effect of finger shadows moving
like raccoons slowly on the still figure of my relaxed
insignificant self.

New Year's, Montpelier, 1885

The river frozen and the striped tent
pegged to the ice next to the mutton-chopped

concentration of four men climbing ladders
down a pyramid of oak barrels they doused

with kerosene under the nearly
full moon, milky way, and Cassiopeia.

Under the tent, while the railroad-spike-
thin mayor punishes the organ, the whole town

around the ice-sculpted swan feasts on cinnamon-
spiced joints of beef, sweetmeats, and a punch

so overcome with Boston rum everyone's cheeks
are flushed and dancing in the insane

swarm of candle lanterns and the quick-shadows
of the night. The bloodshot

dog pack, running a deer through a drift,
look up from their kill at the bonfire

and screams of revelers circle dancing
and teasing the wind sweeping in

like a Gulf Stream from Connecticut. Sparks leap
over the tent. The organ falls

through ice breaking, and the town,
delighted to drift and sway over the dam

of one year into an early thaw, pushes off
into a dream, out of time and silent

as the formally dressed figure in the stern
of a birch canoe passes a jug

to a young woman dipping a paddle
into the quick water becoming the gray

maroon ghost of morning, the fog
chilled and hovering over the smoke

and embers, the new day.

Welcome to the Encyclopedia of Thieves

Pretend this cool and gray suspension
of disbelief is the moon. We're slow dancing

to Chopin in a shallow crater, and you,
wearing the formal attire and moral

superiority of the Christian voodoo,
lift a title for your next book

out of my back pocket,
having borrowed the story line

from your other
and even older brother, no longer

a freshman in college or surprised
at the clandestine liberties

you take, high-stepping
up the rungs of his spine to the desired

and careening heights of your career, slowly
spiraling with a semi-

silent partner across the Sea
of Serenity, where,

like a military
junta in the snows of a Peruvian alp,

we reverse our positions
and you lead, enumerating

the petty thefts of my mood and poetry. We bow
to each other and step to the bar

for a bourbon and water and a small gin.
You flip the record, crank the machine,

and we raise our eyes to the roundhouse
penny arcade of a planet that once

imagined us as the moon-eyed
blossoming of Spring Beauties. Your best friend

in Poughkeepsie, a South American ex-
alcoholic marksman of the short story,

is listening
carefully to the celestial

music of his evening at the kitchen table, turning
the handle of a pencil sharpener,

like an organ grinder, and trying to see
through the familiar and fatal

blind spot into his surprise
published in your name, already in the stars.

Eating the Angel of Death on Mt. Katahdin

Pull the shade, fill the tub, let your headache
slide through the year of the medium

like a stingray gliding into the blood-streaked
white of your third eye scanning

a resurrection of past lives
walking backwards off a cliff on their way to the bank.

Have a nightcap in a spray of rose light, while Black Forest
clockmakers build cuckoos into the night. She loves me.

She loves me not, my bedroll open to anything
that comes along: Meteorites over the mountain, or you

with your Mohegan gash of pubic hair reciting
to a chambered nautilus that refuses to go along with your wish.

You wouldn't climb my answer to the Himalayas
rising to meet the monolithic, three-sided

blue knuckle they call The Cathedral. Plastic flowers
from a graveyard float in space among serene cadavers.

A Polish mistress to an Italian count
slips from her constellation through an astral tube, lifting me

from Knife's Edge into her wings
that ripple like the northern lights

over moose grazing near Chimney Pond. Scheherazade
recited her long tale to a lonely caliph

while her sister combed her hair and commiserated. I
am telling you of an angel's onyx-dark and gold stained wings,

struck by summer lightning, that wrestle and sing until the
    morning
star suffocates like a firefly in jar. I love you.

I love the death
winds of Katahdin. Medium in a trance

reminded you that in the past I've changed. Lilies
are white. Violets are a violent blue and only

those who surrender in the webbed hollows of Cathedral Trail
can understand your elf with a glass rose pinched between my
    teeth.

Don't forget to pick up the bath mat. Sweet dreams.

My Uncle Brian's Concession

A spaniel barks at a heavyset, elegant
man in tweed in his middle years crossing
the bowstring girder bridge rising out of the brown
scar between Ohio and another state. He looks up

at another smoking a small cigar
taking his after-dinner stroll down river street; looks down
at the blue calligraphy of the poem circumnavigating
his cuff, then turns

the corner into a restaurant. In a long
handwritten hello that is nothing much he advises
the missus that after several years he has just
seen his brother. Tap. Tap. Who's there? Someone

small and inquiring what a father in a square room
does without scratching, a fire, or a dog-eared
encyclopedia sprawled across his lap. One hears,
he says, like a bowling alley proprietor

alone at night, the sound of the ideal ball careening
down the edge of boards waxed to the perfection
of imagination toward one pin. Out of this light
to dark brown study one hears a knock. Thirty years

disappear. Who's there? Cheap John the Barker
bringing my fist down between the toboggan
slide and the wheel of fortune before a gathering
of swingers around the little w Stevens sideshow

extravaganza. Under this flap, ladies and gentlemen,
sits the only hundred-year-old ventriloquist
dummy in the States who inhales fire and ice cream, simul-
taneously picking the cashews out of your pocket, joyriding

up the wall of death. Charming the bowels
out of the fat lady chained to the roller coaster,
he'll twirl into such a trance, never seen before
by mortal eyes, ballooning off the high ladder

into a tumble, a tank, a tank of clotted cream that is
the wet, subliminal dream of death for all comers, who pays
their money and takes their chances with the Helen
of Troy vendor of passion frozen in her tracks, until

he breaks the sandwich man on stilts' arched
blue reflection and takes a breath.

Northern Lights

Farmer Manosh liked his beer
and small reputation for turning
a phrase among intimates, their knees
situated under a game of chance, mugs
and pipes filled with smoldering

dark Virginia leaf. At midnight,
July, sixteen hundred
and ninety-one, he rose
from the bench to relieve himself
under the Milky Way in a trench

behind the bakery. When he turned
away from the busines at hand, a woman
with auburn hair appeared, by candlelight,
to be pressing currants into a cake.
Tea breads rising along the walls

like miniature coffins in a mausoleum,
he quickly entered the humidity, and,
with moderate success, after
lifting her apron and dress, after lowering
several more or less distinguished

undergarments, he was having his cake,
when, with a primitive
whalebone rolling pin, she began to smooth
the wave of his hair fallen over the red
eruption of his nose

to the cove at the rear of his cranium.
Outraged, he withdrew to the local
constabulary's chambers, complaining
of an assault, gratuitous and nearly
the end of his game, by a Mistress

Goody of York—handed up before His Honor
and fined an amount appropriate
to her crime. Whether
she paid, willingly, or refused in favor
of having her ankles and wrists locked

into the stocks while Manosh and neighbors
circled around her solitude,
everyone, in a hundred and fourteen
variations on the outcome, tells
a story of a different color. If she paid

(1) in the coin of the realm, did Manosh
have a vision become legend
over dice and ale and passed like a Bible
through generations, where Goody
came to him white as flour and wearing a pastry

apron that she begged him to taste;
or,
if she chose, (2), the humiliation,
did he swallow his tongue and almost
die under a cloud-covered

sliver of moon? If you chose (1),
it is the last thing you remember; if (2),
     dress warmly and hurry
to (3); if you can't decide,
or refuse to cooperate, give us a tale

about a hermaphrodite escaping on ice skates
from enemies on Lake Champlain. (3):
Goody's arms surround Manosh tobogganing
under an ice-covered pine that bridges
Snow Hill. She introduces a thin blade

of sunrise between the third and fourth vertebrae
of his winter coat. Near the foot

of the hill, she tumbles into the point
and their blood
becomes the aurora around the heart of the whole

world without end. Amen.

*Premature Elegy
by Firelight*

The Story of My Life

With a tweezers, chopsticks, and a miniaturized
printing press, I built a book of poems inside a bottle,
floated it in my tub, then to a publisher, who launched

a thousand-bottle campaign from a barge with caviar
and champagne that washed up on the beach of Northumberland,
hobby shops and occupational therapy units

of state mental hospitals. The Navy
modeled a depth charge after it and the FBI
assigned agents to guard me while I played goalie

and put out a line of lingerie
called Spanish Armada. Kneecaps jerked at Doubleday
when several editors dropped their shredders

to flush a manuscript out of the slush pile
into bottles of Tylenol. There were lines
breaking into flames at the perfume counters. Reverend Moon

converted to Judaism. Called to the White House,
the President showed me around the glass of water
where he sunk his teeth. Mother was thrilled. Wife and child

abandoned me to little magazines no longer ready
to print my poems or review my books. I bought a defunct
    volcano
from the Japanese. Raised my coconuts and consciousness.

Hearing of my piety and high vibrations, primal screamers
fashioned a boat out of Perrier bottles and a discarded
Mercedes. They brought me a poster

of Allen Ginsberg blowing a kiss to Ram Dass. Deutsche
Grammophon and Venetian glass blowers were flown in to record
me playing nose flute with pigeon feather and clearing my throat

at Carnegie Hall in a red white and blue Pierre Cardin.
I recited Ovid to a cage of chickadees
while feathering my instrument. To prevent a war

I was deported to the other side, but the KGB
suspected as much and posted me to Paris as set designer
for a Polish luau. I defected

to the cellars of Baron Rothschild. Over dinner
on his yacht, the Mediterranean, like the pale tablecloth,
was so finely woven I could have picked it up by the corners

and pulled it out from under the Baron's eyes
without disturbing the duck press, or that red
pepper of a sun anchored in the horizon. We struck a bargain

that's now history. In Istanbul, an unsuccessful
cataract operation marooned me in a monastery garden,
where I traveled astrally to Siberia and Shaker Heights, living

almost forever. And that's the story of my life.

A Late Twentieth Century
Afternoon with the Dead

It began in late June racing
the sunrise into a fairy ring of orange

cornucopia mushrooms across the path
to a pitcher plant and orchid-

speckled bog that surrounded a swimming hole, blue
filtering through angel cake

bog soil into a brook slowly
twisting around dark

yellow birch, mint, and pine needles so sweet
they put you to sleep. I woke

from a dream of wheels sparking under black
smoking engines rushing to collide

and found myself face to face with a tribunal
of porcupines. Hissing

monk scribes out of the dark ages
come back on all fours. A sharp quill

of certainty flowered out of every pore, the shallow
caves behind them squinting

like the eyes of hell in sunlight. I was about to reach
for my clothes draped over a branch when a sudden

display of quills and blood
colored the air accompanied by two

thirty ought six explosions I followed to the wrist
of someone half-hiding in the green

haze of a shrub as two more
shells slid into chambers aimed

at my erection's periscoping little half-life
all its own. I felt a light breeze

picking up and said, over my
embarrassment, I fell asleep

after swimming. I reached
for my jeans but a woman's voice

said put your hands where they belong.
This is my land and that's my

blue spruce. Dead or otherwise,
you're trespassing.

Personal Holiday

I returned from the emergency
operation just in time to overhear
you telling Papa he was being replaced
by one whose golf handicap was so low
you could walk on it, dragging me
across the street or squeezing welts
into my neck as he and you cursed and tore
your way out of adultery, that new idea, into what

would surface, in thirty years, as a point of view: daughter
leaves husband, son leaves wife, and I, the eldest,
follow suit. Remember
the barber's son, his khakis
to his knees, feet apart in poison ivy, who thought
I should learn to masturbate over the leaves. And who
can forget your lawyer's
formal attire: Papa's, all green

tobacco leaves and drool
roaring his tits off—yours, temporarily
employed to uncover which one of you
I loved, not quite a teenager, above the other. He fooled
with the dial of the hearing aid, while Papa
and you, secreted behind the door, tumbled
into each other as I charged
the street where Papa's idea

of a private eye was reliving his years
of public service into a handkerchief. My Latin teacher
said I could make up for the work I missed.
My girlfriend kissed another guy. Recuperating
in the urology wing, I practiced
my bar mitzvah speech as my gentile
roommate died of emphysema,
listening. Years later, in the corridor

of the resort motel, Papa threatened to cut me
out of his will to change
my mind about monogamy, telling my wife
about a gumshoe he would hire to tail
me and the new woman in my life. Some of the old ones
were first cousins, maids, and your mysteriously
reappearing heart like a tempered

glass door revolving between hell and Alaska.
Your daughter told me
you can't hear my name. Neither can I. Rupert.
Rondeau. Rodney. Rondell. Ellen
is the reason. I love someone
you'll never meet. Hold on
to the one you did as I let go
of you and Papa cursing each other's

parents walking the aisle of skullcaps
bobbing and beards over mouths babbling mucusy
incantations toward my brief
bar mitzvah speech. The rabbi, still breathing
out of great yellow nostrils, blessed me quick.
Your other son in a bow tie thought it a lark
and crossed himself on the way to the schnapps
and honey cake. Here in Vermont

there's a fire dancing
its blue head off in the open stove
putting its tongue where it pleases. Papa
in Palm Beach takes a nine iron
for a chip out of the rough and you're
filling shelves for the Chistmas rush
on running-bras and panties embossed
with little sayings to push

the man in her life through his day, not unlike
"metrical literacy" or the new
criteria. Brother wrote with joy,

after speaking to his wife with the flat of his hand,
of giving old cars a new life, wondering whether
to hate his father or smoke a joint. Sister,
over the phone, sounded uneasy out of marriage,
like one of the shivering young formalists

trying to cross against the light
without collar stays, license, or a metronome. And we all
ran after our father's wife, leaving Papa
out of the family portrait, free to choose an iron-
spined young widow so intent on cutting him
out of your maternal sphere—little girl,
second son, and black sheep number one—she succeeded

with Papa under her thumb who chose a deaf
and dumb retreat from the souvenirs
and shrapnel of your enlightened
parentage. These days
I write and teach and love a woman
who loves me back. In '55 you surprised
the cold war–era east side of town with brushfire
news of your adultery. Surprise but no crime.
It caught on. Wives that stayed married

went to work for wives that didn't. The men,
divorced or not, lost themselves in the creeks
and sand traps and watched the news, one hand draped
around a Heineken. Years pass. Your daughter falls
out of marriage with your ideal: golf buff
in red alpaca knit, well-to-do, a safe bet

these days—who could argue while falling asleep
or taking a long one from your second son's sinsemilla-
filled calabash. His ex-wife was not
your kind of sport. She loved the sauce
and testicles under a quilt
like no one else could and you were pleased
with her departure. Which brings me
to me continuing to feed the running diatribe

under a hair dryer, your neighbor
listening hard, while the blind manicurist's
emery board's sense of repetition
and sound curves your thumbnail
toward a fine and lacquered point. Mother,
your grandchildren are well enough and cared for,
but our love's nothing more
than imagining you gritting your teeth,
hating me or yourself, what's the difference.

Invisible Fire

*Visible fire lives just as long
as it has nourishment.*—Heraclitus

Loitering at the outskirts of the walnut-paneled
Hall of Bankruptcy, I paced the shallows
of a white marble river that fell into a pool
of lawyers and their customers. My sandals
in my purse, my eyes a little bruised
from last night, I quickly passed the glass-covered
Directory of courts and judges, where I caught
the reflection of my long
blond hair, nylons, and a dark blue suit
avoiding the mainstream, looking back
through the intertwined and struggling
red and white worms impaled in dung-colored irises.
I accelerated, moving
even closer to the folded canvas hose and copper
extingusher behind glass, the cut
crystal doorknobs to rooms without numbers,
names—she always (talking
to herself or me) wanted to hold or push
anyone at the brink. I brushed my hand
like a blind woman reading epitaphs across the illegible
lives on plaques, their dates embossed
and passing the gauntlet of one death
to another under bronze mustaches. I kneeled to myself
as a little girl, and with my finger shaking, I adjusted
the thick tortoise-shell glasses, her skin
white as sweet marjoram
scented dough, and said no, I'm sorry
I'm crying, and pushed through glass doors to the hot cement
where I was born—Mother, may I—to a cool customer
who kept her shoes on, scrubbing
the same dress, same child, until there
was no dress, no child, and nothing more to say: She
in me, like that folded hose swelling with the cold

currents of the underground breaking, breaking me
down and down into my element, and I rushed us both
into the nearsighted blur of horns and brakes, and nothing
happened. Nothing.

Everytime You Say Yes It's an Indictment of the Last Six Months of My Life

Because the woman gouges sand
with a fish bone; because the man reaches
for a dog's ear flopping

on its way to a sea bird already in flight;
because the idea of rain freezing on the bare
branch of winter is miles away; and because
you and I are equally lonely in mild love

or hate, what the hell. Let's fly the weekend
to a Virgin Islands mosquito farm, dance awhile
to the red hum of the future, drink wine

with fruit and back-float in the cool
turquoise, harming not even ourselves,
then settle into the side effects
of separate lives, join hands

to raise our children above disaster
and talk like friends or enemies when we need to.

Water Music

There lived a man who suffocated
the mouth of a tobacco jar with a clean
handkerchief, then tipped the corpse, leaving
his wife for another and other lands. This red-eyed
pilgrim was only a little bald, not
that tall, drunk, or that fair
to look upon. He had better things to do

like open a can of deviled ham,
fry an egg over it, and call it supper, coveting
fine instruments, not for the way
they mitered a corner or tightened the string
of a gold lute—life was brandy-
soaked tobacco smoke. Red snapper whickered
and swam into his hands. Coconuts

fell and split on his machete, silver and by his side
like a wolfhound or a new bride. Bathed
in sunlight, the wind purred through the turquoise
threads of his hammock, palm fronds
and jasmine strewn across his path.
He stole a boat and whispered
across waves slapping that he couldn't survive

without the blue-smoking tongue of a wife
to tell him this or that or where to put it. Rolling

off the kitchen table, his children
loved him as children love to cool their feet
in a tidepool or tall grass. One morning
in the season of thick moss, pine
needles and ferns steaming, another

and even younger man, without consulting
the knowhow of his old crony, folded a sausage
and cheese into the inner life of a napkin
tied to a stick and left *his* wife. What kind of a general
delivery how-do-you-do do you think he received
months later and out of the blue from his mentor
his old friend—I could end it here.

You could have a beer, unfasten your belt, look
to the title, think the worst or wonder
what kind of a primrose cul-de-sac
is this bardic fool giving us
this time. Keep your pants on. Such an enterprise
has two purposes: You enter the war zone
of your own contrary forces, searching

the swampy regions to better understand
your own defenses; then, once you've reconnoitered
this terrain (its arbors and mists) and found a familiar
patch of jack-in-the-pulpit and stinkhorns, fall back
and roll around and reminisce about
that cold marriage or kiss
that changed your life. It's here in a relentless

pursuit of pain or pleasure that you
can easily get a purchase on what it's like
to brag to another, turn her over, complain,
keep it to yourself or pass it on. My tale
is done. I like a reader who sits
on his wristwatch and it relaxes me
to imagine him opening the zipper of his purse

after he's finished without being asked. Bless him
for his hearty wine and may his enemies
kiss both cheeks, on the run and after
a preacher after a poacher—whosoever

catches their drift will marry my daughter
or make himself scarce forever, wherever
the morning after is rancid milk

on a thick tongue and the wind
tattoos rain against the windowpane.

Premature Elegy by Firelight

I never had the time to write
about the loneliness of waking
at 4 A.M. to the certainty of my own
early demise in my father's eye

that wrote me off like a painless
new surgery for cataracts. I never
had a minute until my brother's cat
that ate the canary grin drove all day

through a storm with a loaf of bread
and the image of the two of us
on our backs and staring at the heartbeat
of fire punishing the ceiling until daybreak

erased everything we knew our father
never let us close to. We didn't
do that. He had business
further north and I had already

invented a new father better than my own
who was just as lonely as the son
he had invented to keep him company
for the last minutes of moonlight before morning.

It's Like That

People in love only talk about themselves, you say
and abandon a sock and a shoe overnight in a pot, dreaming
I'm snow and you're wind
whipped pine needles scratching the bark and pitch
and wake to the red-winged, one-eyed shadow
over your spine that dips into the rise
of your lower back. I throw the bone-
shaped alarm clock to the dog and slide
into the phosphorescent
undertow, arched and squeezing the embalmed
years of sensibility out of my agitated
screaming out of the ceiling, like divorce
on a ferris wheel and suffocate it
slowly into the sheets. Or take the impossible
blue of a dragonfly, quick and dodging
its reflection on a lake after the fog
has given in to the pale
moon of morning and throw that
into the logic of the sock and the shoe
and you'll understand why I love you.
It's like that.